Lamps of the

Jan Lindenberger

4880 Lower Valley Road, Atglen, PA 19310 USA

Designed by Laurie Smucker

ISBN: 0-7643-0355-4
Printed in China

Published by Schiffer Publishing Ltd.
4880 Lower Valley Road
Atglen, PA 19310
Phone: (610) 593-1777; Fax: (610) 593-2002
E-mail: Schifferbk@aol.com
Please write for a free catalog.
This book may be purchased from the publisher.
Please include $3.95 for shipping.
Try your bookstore first.

We are interested in hearing from authors
with book ideas on related subjects.

Contents

Acknowledgments

A very special thank you to Myke Johnson from 50/Fiftys Antiques for allowing me to come to her home to photograph her vast collection. The majority of the lamps in this book are from her shop and her home. Myke deals in 50s/60s collectibles and furniture. Her patience in arranging and rearranging her home is greatly appreciated. Another special thanks to Bill and Kristi Lewis for the large contribution from their home and shop. Bill and Kristi are specialized dealers in 50s/60s antiques at their shop, Spotlight on Modern, in the Antique Center, Denver, Colorado. Also thanks to Doni Brune for her special added touch. And to anyone else whom I may have forgotten.

50/Fifty featured at Mountain Man Antiques, Denver, Colorado
Antique Mart of Elk Grove, Illinois
Bill and Kristi Lewis, Spotlight on Modern, Denver, Colorado
De'Ja'Vu, St. Joseph, Missouri
Magpie Antiques, Elk Grove, Illinois
Your Quest Ends Here Antique Mall, Granger, Indiana
Johnnie Mae Gipe, St. Joseph, Missouri
Darlene Schaake, Antique Center on Broadway, Denver, Colorado
Bill Kieffert, Denver, Colorado
Tammie and Roger Sawicki, Denver, Colorado
Top Value Stamp Catalog. Top Value Enterprises, Inc.
   N.Y, N.Y. 1956
Living Magazine. September, 1961. N.Y, N.Y.
Spiegel Catalog. Spring & summer, 1962. Chicago, Ill.
Montgomery Ward Catalog. 1969. Kansas City, Mo.

Introduction

You light up my life!

What can one say about these lamps that are "so bad, they're good?"

Chances are, you will recognize quite a few of these kitchy items from the 1940s through the early 1970s and wonder what ever inspired anyone to design, let alone buy and decorate their homes with these lamps.

While the utility of a lamp in the home is quite obvious, design and decorating are something else again. The thoroughly modern 1950s housewife, wanting to implement art and modern design into her household, found a natural outlet for this urge in lighting. Designers offered all manner of scientific patterns such as amoeba, starburst, and atomic styles to reflect the postwar mood. Additionallly, new materials and production techniques developed during the war era were readily available for new commercial purposes. All of these forces collided to create the lamps we hate to love. But love them we do. How could we pass up a "Rembrandt," with its stylized shade atop a brass ball trapped in a black steel base? To us, these lamps represent an era of hope, modernism, and faith that science and technology had stepped in to create a bright future for the hardworking American family.

Take the T.V. lamp for example. Born of the concern over eyesight damage from the modern contraption which so fascinated the American family, the T.V. lamp sought to alleviate middle class discomfort about the dangers of television viewing. Taking advantage of television's new flat surface, no ethnic group or member of the animal kingdom was overlooked by the modern housewife with a flair for decorating. You could visit the depths of the ocean, darkest Africa, or far away China, simply by turning on your T.V. lamp. If you had a green thumb, you could buy a T.V. lamp that doubled as a planter. And some planter T.V. lamps even came with a package of planter mix. Adding to the proliferation of T.V. lamps, many companies threw in a lamp with the purchase of a new television set.

Not content with stationary T.V. lamps, the action lamp was resurrected for those who desired a little more excitment in the living room decor. Action lamps had been around since the 1920s, depicting such scenes as Niagara Falls, forest fires, trains, and buses. Hopalong Cassidy, from the 1950s, is among the most valuable and sought after of these lamps. Other popular novelty lamps of the era include fish bowl styles, motorized hula dancers, angel fish swimming around a clock face. A truly kitchy example has to be the phone-clock-cigarette lighter combination with venetian blind shade.

For a "blast from the past" we always enjoy a 1960s cult favorite, the Lava Lite. The advertisement for the classic Century model promised a "motion for every emotion." The Century is still being produced today, but the older originals can be identified by the screw-on caps. For fun, hippies also indulged themselves with the rarer Spaceship, Aladdin-style and Coach Lantern lamps too. Not to be left out, the Japanese even got in on the fad with a highly collectible cylindrical T.V. lamp knockoff of the Lava Lite.

Today, lamps are fun collectibles, relatively inexpensive and easy to find, and they can add a humorous touch to any decorating scheme. The examples in this book are some of the best (and worst) we could dig up, but there are hundreds of styles out there to light up your life. We hope this book will "turn you on" to lamps.

I hope you take this lamp handbook and price guide, with you on your lamp buying trips and use it to find just the right light!

Prices are based upon my personal observations and may differ from coast to coast. Auction prices may differ from shop prices. Prices are also affected by condition and availability.

Table Lamps

Brass, Metal, & Wood

Ceramic and brass with fiberglass shade and starburst bulb. $95-150

Brass designers table lamp with fiberglass shades. 24". $75-150

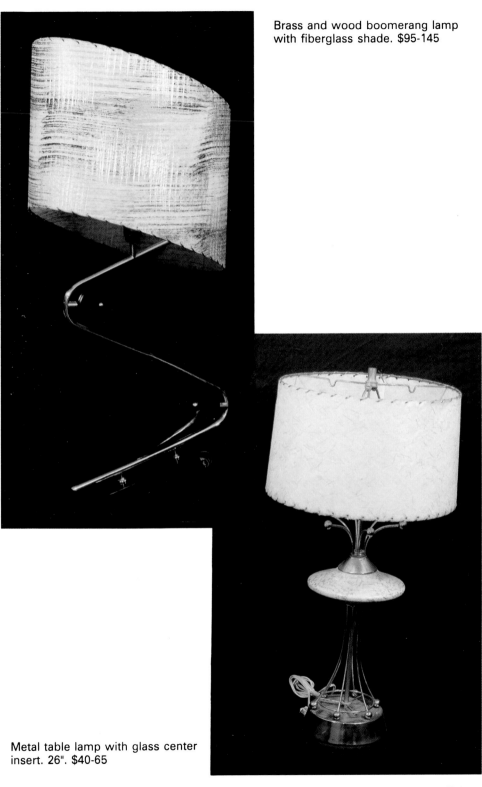

Brass and wood boomerang lamp with fiberglass shade. $95-145

Metal table lamp with glass center insert. 26". $40-65

9

Wood and brass
boomerang lamp with
fiberglass shade. 26".
$130-200 pair

Brass S-shaped table
lamp with double
fiberglass shades.
$95-125

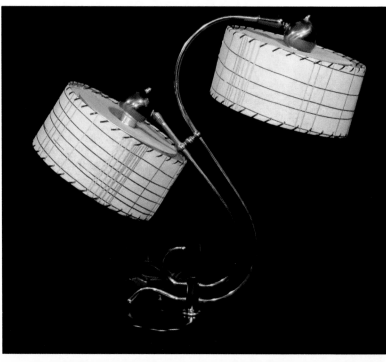

Polished brass table lamp with half moon-shaped wood design and fiberglass leaf shape shade. $125-200

Spun fiberglass shade on metal poles and base. Table lamp. 60". $80-110

Metal spiral table lamp with cardboard shade. 24"-30". $75-150

12

Wooden design with marble base. 22". $15-20

Brass and painted metal table lamp, plastic flowers in base with fiberglass shade. 31". $55-75

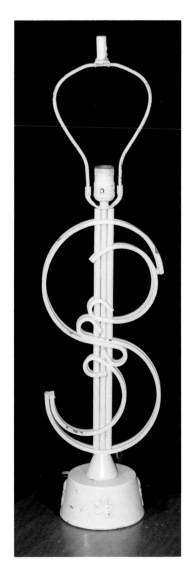

Iron dollar sign lamp. 18". $30-40

Brass table lamp. $45-65

15

Wood and brass table lamp with cloth
shades. $55-75

Brass spiral table lamp with cardboard shade. $25-45

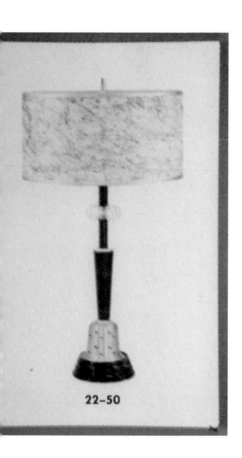

22-50

Black and brass base with white veiling fiberglass shade. Oxford. 17". $35-65. Top Value stamp catalog, no. 22-50.

Palm table lamp with fiberglass shade. 40". $200-400 pair

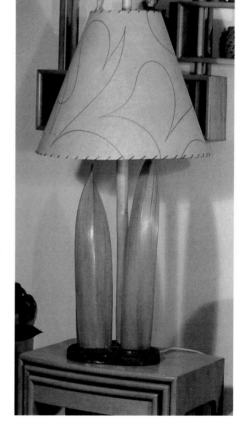

Wooden designer's table lamp. 40".
Fiberglass shade. 27". $45-65

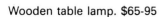

Wooden table lamp. $65-95

18

Wood tabie lamp. 18". $25-35

Wood with metal base table lamp.
Atomic design on top. 21". $80-100
pair

19

Wood and brass boomerang lamp with double fiberglass shade. 30". $75-150

Black metal wing design table lamp.
16". $18-25

Pink fiberglass shade on brass spiral lamp. 25". $100-200

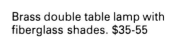

Brass double table lamp with fiberglass shades. $35-55

Table lamp with green glass design and brass spindles. Fiberglass shade. 33". $100-150 each

Clear glass table lamp with cardboard shade. Gold fish design. 31". $100-200 each. $200-400 pair

Ceramic and brass table lamp with
Venetian blind shade. 22". $45-65

Gold trimmed plaster table lamp.
Fiberglass dimensional shade. 28".
$60-75

Brass and iron table lamp. Rembrandt Masterpiece Lamps. 29". $125-150 pair

Plaster

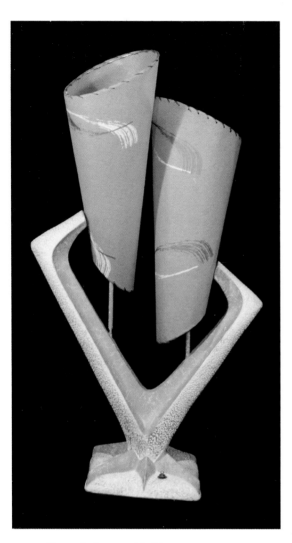

Ceramic lamp with fiberglass shades.
$125-145

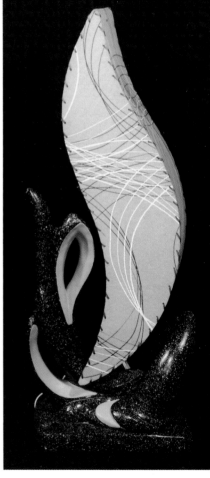

Ceramic T.V. lamp with fiberglass
shade. 28". $125-155

26

Ceramic lamp with fiberglass tiered
shade, starburst light bulbs. 16".
$75-110

Plastic and ceramic designer's lamp
with fiberglass shade. 31.5". $65-95.
Top Value stamp catalog, no. 22-8.
1956.

22-8

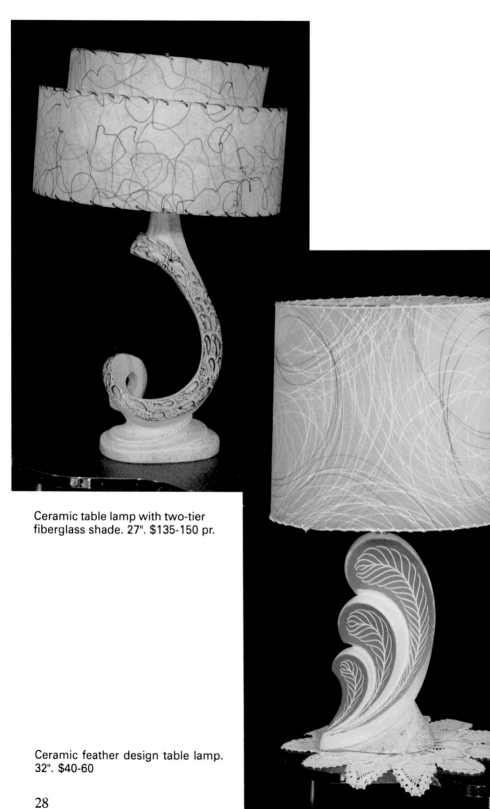

Ceramic table lamp with two-tier
fiberglass shade. 27". $135-150 pr.

Ceramic feather design table lamp.
32". $40-60

28

Ceramic table lamp with fiberglass shade. 24". $130-150 pair

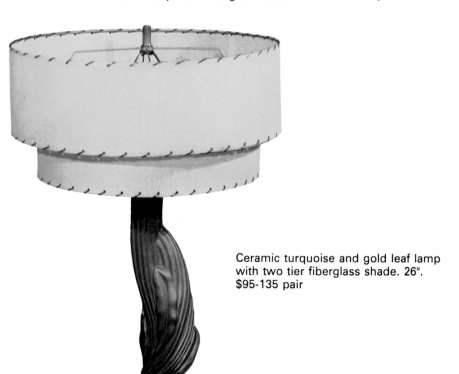

Ceramic turquoise and gold leaf lamp with two tier fiberglass shade. 26". $95-135 pair

29

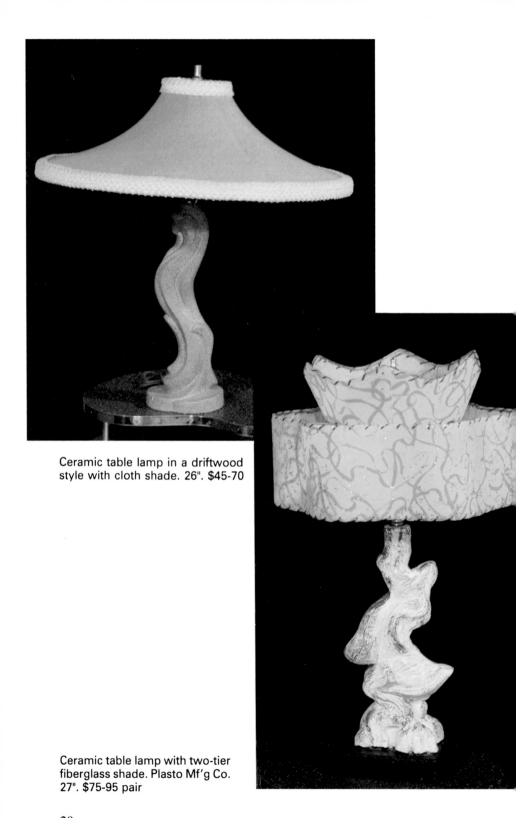

Ceramic table lamp in a driftwood style with cloth shade. 26". $45-70

Ceramic table lamp with two-tier fiberglass shade. Plasto Mf'g Co. 27". $75-95 pair

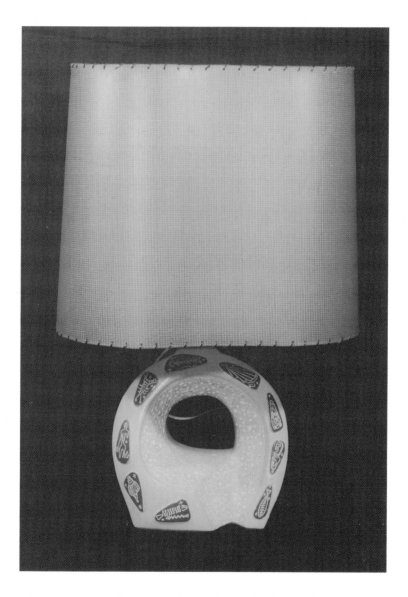

Ceramic horse shoe-shape lamp. Paper shade. 14". $110-140 pair

Ceramic ballet dancer lamp with a wrong shade. 20". $45-55

Ceramic victorian couple table lamp. The shade is wrong. 26". $45-65

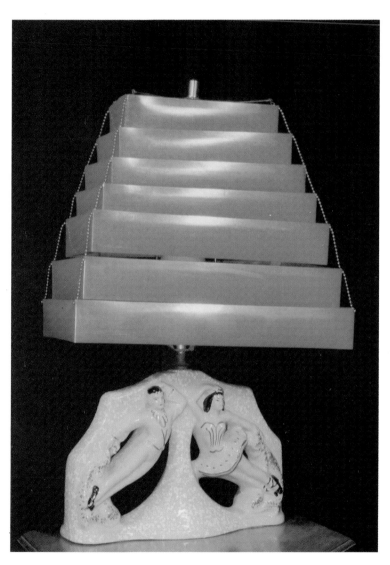

Ceramic ballet dancers lamp. The shade is not original. $35-55

Fiberglass triple shade table lamp. Lucite base with ceramic revolving lady. Moss. 38". $300-600

Lucite base with fiberglass upper
section and shade. $95-150

Lucite floor lamp. Moss. 60". $375-450

Lucite lamps with silk shades. 19". $40-45 each

Lucite table lamp. Moss. 24". $300-500 pair. It came as a three-piece set. 2 table lamps and 1 floor.

36

Orange paper lantern style T.V. lamp. 16". $12-20

Plastic and wood desk lamp. 15".
$15-25

Plastic light bulb table lamp. 23". $65-130

Atomic chrome table lamp. 17". $90-110

Glass ball table lamp. 1970s. 12".
$125-250

Table lamp with aluminum circular base and glass globe on top. $85-140

Ceramic

Ceramic gazelle table lamp with fiberglass shade. 30". $95-125

Ceramic floral lamp with paper shade. $110-145 pair

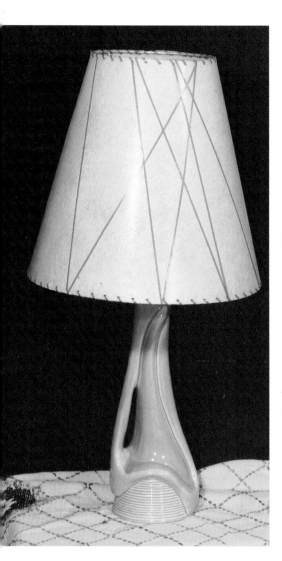

Ceramic table lamp. Fiberglass shade.
32". $35-65

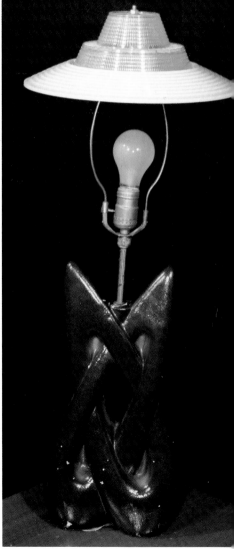

Ceramic green table lamp. (Wrong
shade). 14". $25-35

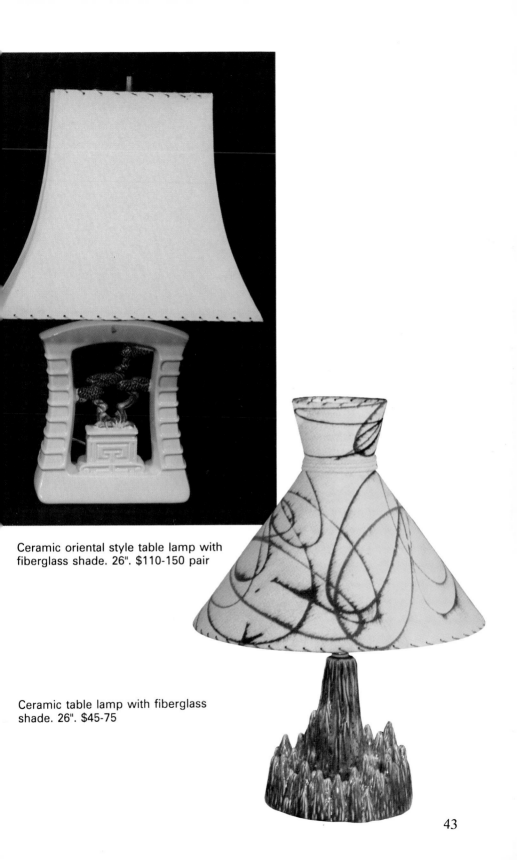

Ceramic oriental style table lamp with fiberglass shade. 26". $110-150 pair

Ceramic table lamp with fiberglass shade. 26". $45-75

43

Ceramic woman table lamp. $40-75

Ceramic panther lamp with fiberglass shade. 27". $65-85

Ceramic oriental table lamp with fiberglass shade. 26". $35-55

Ceramic basket table lamp/planter.
Paper shade. 22". $45-55

Ceramic table lamp with leaf design.
Fiberglass shade. 29". $35-55

46

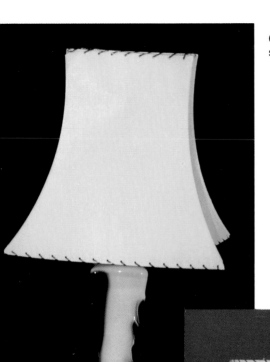

Ceramic table lamp with fiberglass shade. 32". $55-75

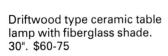

Driftwood type ceramic table lamp with fiberglass shade. 30". $60-75

47

Ceramic table lamp. 8" tall. $15-25

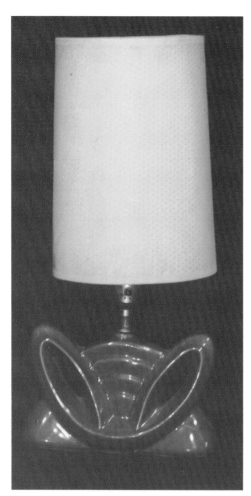

Ceramic cactus table lamp with cone shaped fiberglass shade. 24". $35-55

Ceramic table lamp with floral insert. Fiberglass shade. $45-75

Ceramic and plastic table lamp with fiberglass shade. 26". $45-60

Ceramic gold and black table lamp. Fiberglass shade. 18". $45-60

50

Brass and ceramic table lamp with two-tier paper shade. 24". $35-65

Black ceramic table lamp with fiberglass shade. 16". $45-60

Plaster table lamp. Geometric shape with wood top. $40-50

Ceramic gold trimmed table lamp. (Wrong shade). 16". $25-35

Ceramic table lamp. $35-45

Ceramic painted, gold leaf
table lamp, with fiberglass
shade. 27". $35-65

China figurine lamp with gold fiberglass shade. 16". $50-60

Ceramic pink table lamp with fiber-glass shade. 40". $50-60

Ceramic table lamps with gold accents. Fiberglass shades. 20". $30-45 pair

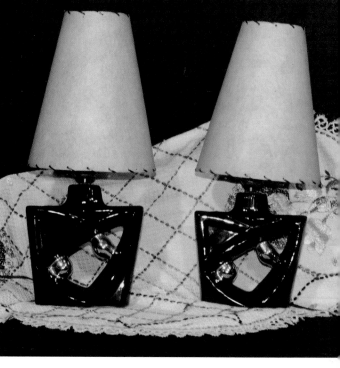

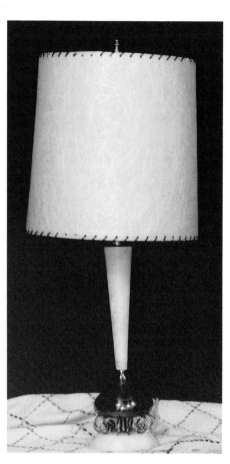

Alabaster and brass table lamp with fiberglass shade. 25". $65-85 pair

Pair of ceramic bedroom lamps. Cardboard shade. 15". $30-40 pair

56

Ceramic crown T.V. light. 12". $35-55

Ceramic T.V. lamp in metal base which doubles as a planter. $25-55

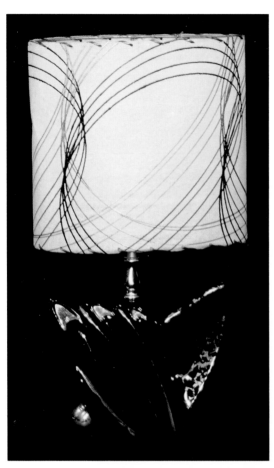

Dresser lamp in black ceramic with gold swirl. Fiberglass shade. 19". $75-110 pair

Ceramic T.V. lamp with glass flowers. 10". $25-50

Traditional

Table lamp in gold leaf on clear frosted glass. Silk shade. 36.5 ". $40-50

Hall china table lamp. Hand painted leaf design on concave china column with a brass base. Rayon shade. 28". $45-65. Top Value stamp catalog. 1956.

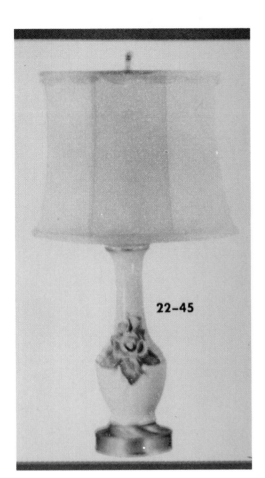

Brass base with china flower design on china lamp. Silk shade. Cordey. 29". $35-50. Top Value stamp catalog, no. 22-45.

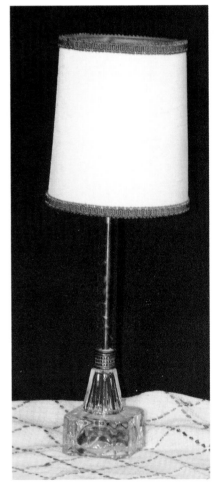

Glass table lamp. Came as a pair. 21". $120-140 pair

Glass table lamp. Came as a pair. 21". $120-140 pair

Etched layered glass table lamp. Silk
shade. 40". $40-50

Ceramic column with climbing vine
table lamp. Paper pleated shade. 32".
$35-45

Hand painted floral glass table lamp with gold accents and brass base. Silk shade. 38". $45-60

Ceramic table lamp with embossed flowers and gold tone base. 26". $30-40

Ceramic table lamp with gold design and trim on brass sculptured base. Paper pleated shade. 29". $30-40

Crystal prisms, with marble and pot metal base table lamp. Silk shade. 44".
$100-120

Animals, Fish, & Birds

Ceramic panther lamp/
planter with fiberglass
shade. 22". $75-95

Glass horses on brass base with glass prisms in the center, T.V. lamp. 11". $70-85

Ceramic panther desk lamp with fiberglass shade. 16". $55-95

Ceramic panther lamp. (Wrong shade). 22". $35-55

Ceramic T.V. lamp of panthers. $45-75

Black panther. T.V. lamp. 1950s. 12". $55-70

Black panther table lamp. 6". $45-65

Ceramic panther T.V. lamp/planter. 10". $35-45

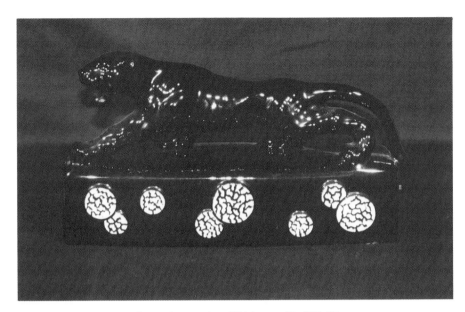

Ceramic panther T.V. lamp. 9". $55-85

Ceramic panther T.V. lamp and planter. 8". $45-60

Ceramic panther T.V. lamp. $45-65

Black ceramic panther with fiberglass shade, T.V. lamp. 10". $50-100

Ceramic boxer T.V. lamp with fiberglass shade. 10". $50-100

Ceramic Dachshund T.V. lamp with fiberglass shade. 10". $50-100

Plaster, dogs, night light. 8". $45-65

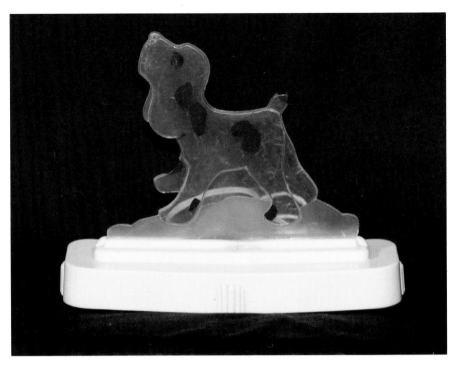

Lucite dog with plastic base T.V. lamp. $50-100

Ceramic poodle on wood base T.V. lamp. Fiberglass shade. 12". $50-100

Pair of plaster poodles, table lamps. Fiberglass shades with felt applied poodles that have rhinestone eyes. 24". $190-225 pair

Ceramic horse speckled with gold design T.V. lamp. 12". $35-55

Plaster rearing horse table lamp. 22". $35-55

22-7

Phil-Mar horse and foal lamp. Ebony ceramic base. Red fiberglass shade. 25". $45-65. Top Value stamp catalog, no. 22-3. 1956.

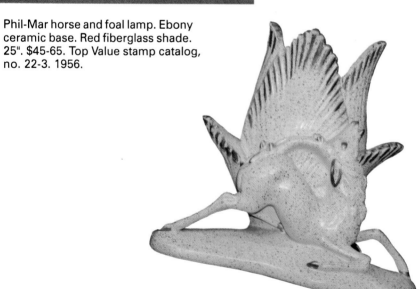

Ceramic gazelle table lamp. $40-50

Ceramic deer T.V. lamp with glass insert. 14". $45-65

Ceramic gazelle T.V. lamp/ planter. Fiberglass shade. 26". $65-85

your library, we would like to keep you informed about other publications from Schiffer Publishing Ltd.

TITLE OF BOOK: _____

☐ hardcover
☐ paperback

☐ Bought at: _____
☐ Received as gift

COMMENTS or ideas for books you would like us to publish. _____

_____

_____

_____

Name *(please print clearly)* _____

Address _____

City _____ State _____ Zip _____

☐ *Please send me a free Schiffer Arts, Antiques & Collectibles catalog.*
☐ *Please send me a free Schiffer Woodcarving, Woodworking & Crafts catalog*
☐ *Please send me a free Schiffer Military/Aviation History catalog*
☐ *Please send me a free Whitford Press Mind, Body & Spirit and Donning Pictorials & Cook books catalog.*

Telephone: (610)-593-1777   Fax: (610)-593-2002   E-mail: Schifferbk@aol.com

SCHIFFER BOOKS ARE CURRENTLY AVAILABLE FROM YOUR BOOKSELLER

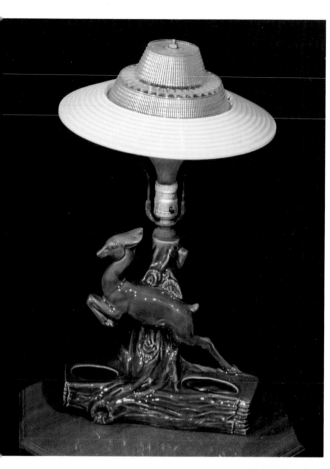

Ceramic gazelle table lamp/planter.
(Wrong shade). 14". $35-50

Ceramic fish and sea shell T.V. lamp.
$35-55

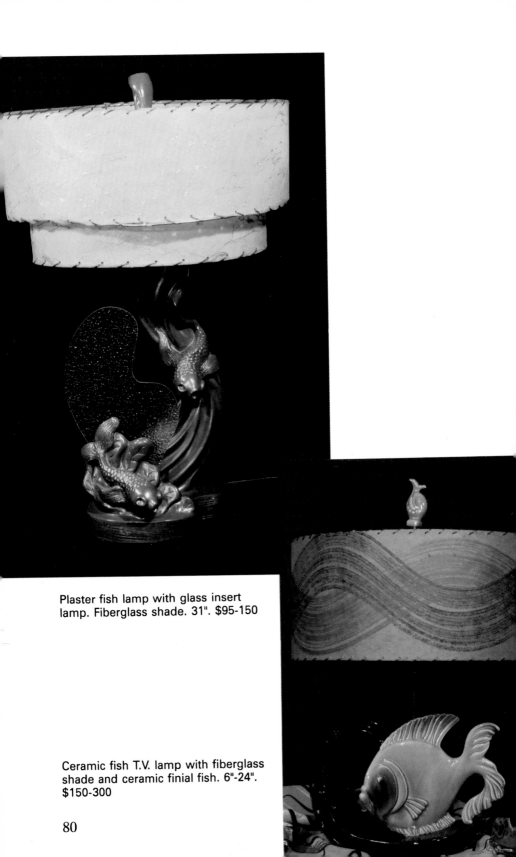

Plaster fish lamp with glass insert
lamp. Fiberglass shade. 31". $95-150

Ceramic fish T.V. lamp with fiberglass
shade and ceramic finial fish. 6"-24".
$150-300

Ceramic fish T.V. lamp.
Lane and Co. Van Ives, Ca.
1957. 14". $60-120

Ceramic sea shell look
table lamp with fish
swimming around base.
Fiberglass shade. 40".
$60-80

Plastic fish T.V. lamp. 8". $35-45

Sea shell lamp with wood base. 8". $20-30

Ceramic deer T.V. lamp 8". $40-50

Ceramic ram T.V. lamp. 14". $40-50

Ceramic duck T.V. lamp and planter. 12". $30-40

Ceramic flying duck T.V. light. 12". $45-65

Ceramic flying duck T.V. light. 14". $55-75

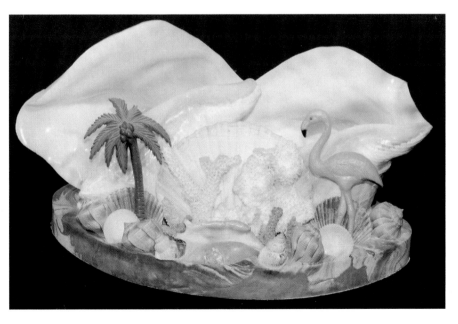

Sea shell T.V. lamp with beach scene. 8". $45-65

Plaster bird on leaf table lamp. Cloth shade. 27". $75-95

Ceramic swan T.V. lamp. Fiberglass back. 10". $40-55

Ceramic swan T.V. lamp. 12". $55-75

Plaster oriental lamp with venetian blind shade. 16". $150-195 pair

Ceramic junk and Chinese couple T.V. lamp. Venetian blind shade. 19". $65-95

Ceramic Chinese people in junk, T.V. lamp. Silk shade. 20". $50-60

Plaster gondola T.V. lamp with fiberglass shade. 10". $35-65

Plaster oriental T.V. lamp with plastic shade. 10". $35-65

Ceramic oriental lady lamp/ planter. 12". $45-60

90

Plaster table lamps. Silk shade.
Oriental man and woman. 38".
$120-140 pair

91

Pagoda planter base lamp. Cold
painted on ceramic with cotton shade.
27". $45-65

Plaster Siam man, one of a pair,
woman not shown. 18". $95-110 pair

Plaster dancing Hawaiian woman with chenille shade. Continental Art Co. 1951. (Came with a male dancer also) $250-500 pair

Wooden aloha table lamp. Red lights in breasts. 19". $75-150

Chalk oriental dancing man and woman table lamps with silk shades. $250-500

Hawaiian woman in boat, T.V. lamp. Ceramic with gold splash paint. 8". $75-150

Plaster Polynesian woman, T.V. lamp.
13". $75-125

Plaster male dancer table
lamp. Came as a pair, with
male and female lamps.
$175-225 pair

Plaster African mask T.V. lamp. 20".
$55-75

Plaster Blackamoor table lamps. 22". $95-150 pr.

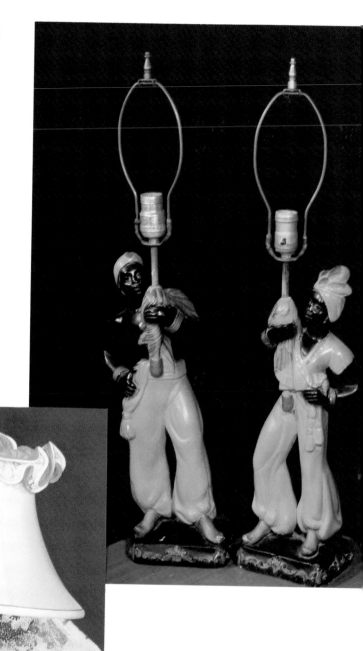

Blackamoor plaster T.V. lamp with silk shade. $80-100

Plaster Blackamoor table lamp with fiberglass and fabric shade. 16". $40-60

Wood and Lucite lamp with ceramic Blackamoor and silk shade. $55-85

98

Animated, Motion, and Clock Lamps

Electric metal lamp with glass insert. Fish swim around clock. 8". $125-150

Pot metal hula woman table lamp with clock insert. Burlap shade and fringed skirt. 22". $400-800

Bakelite and glass neon clock/night light. 6". $150-300

Pot metal hula woman table lamp
with clock insert. Burlap shade
and fringed skirt. 22". $400-800

Lava Lite (Aladdin-style), brass
and wrought iron. Phased out
in 1977. 14". $60-95

Waterfall scene, motion lamp. Metal with plastic shade. 11". $110-145

Brass Lava Lite with original box.
Century Classic. Circa 1965. Still
being produced today. 17". $75-110

Glass and brass Lava Lite. Flower
ring. 16". $45-75

Ceramic bulb-style lamp and clock to match. Clock: 7.5"; lamp: 12.5". $75-110 pair

Ceramic bird set lamp. Lights up from back. 22". $95-125

Ceramic clock lamp with venetian blind shade. 26". $65-95

Floor Lamps

Iron floor lamp with African mask (different face on each side) in center. Fiberglass shade. 58". $175-300

Double fiberglass shade, metal floor lamp. 60". $175-300

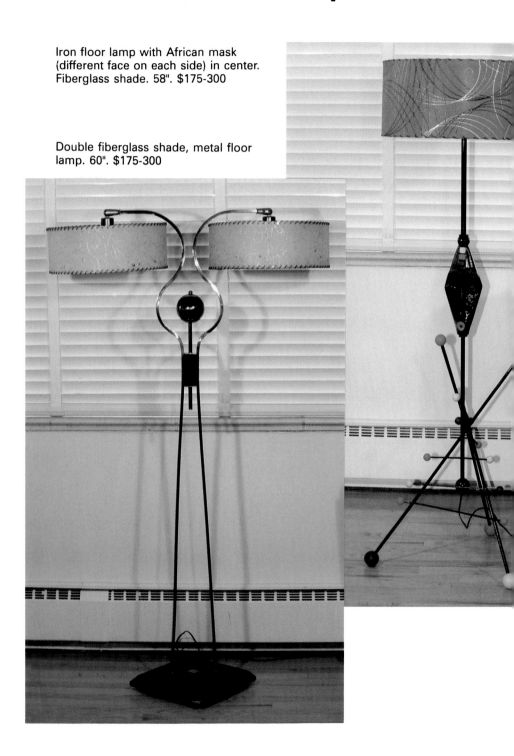

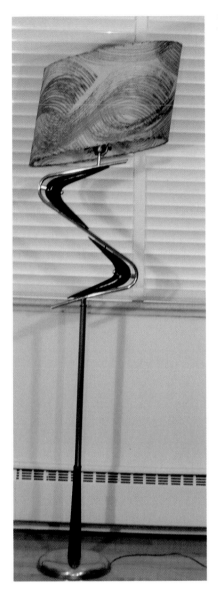

Swirl design brass floor lamp with fiberglass shade. 67". $150-300

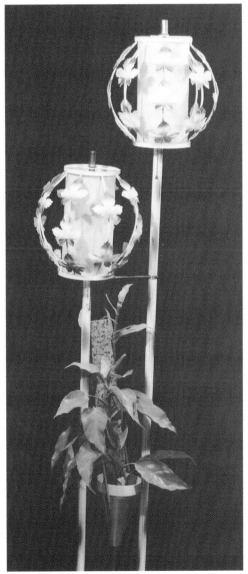

Metal leaves on circular globes with twisted pole stem, floor lamp. Metal shade inside. Planter/lamp. 60". $60-100

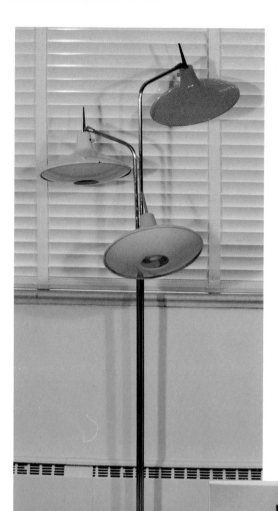

Metal floor lamp with disk shades. 65". $150-300

Left to right: Four in one combination wrought iron lamp. Ash tray, magazine rack, table and lamp. 50". $60-80. Double goose neck brass plated trim on base and bullet shades. 61". $75-95. Tole floor lamp with metal leaf decorated shade. 61". $40-65. Goose neck brass floor lamp with linen shade. 18". $35-60. Top Value stamp catalog product numbers shown. 1956.

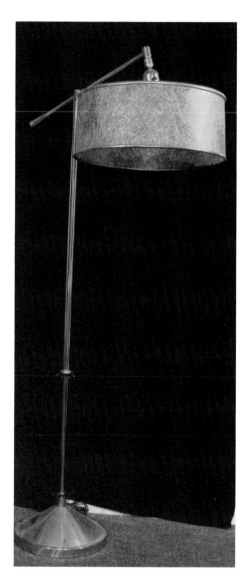

Brass and wrought iron floor lamp.
Fiberglass shade. 60". $55-75

Brass and metal floor lamp with
fiberglass 2 tier fiberglass shade. 60".
$110-150

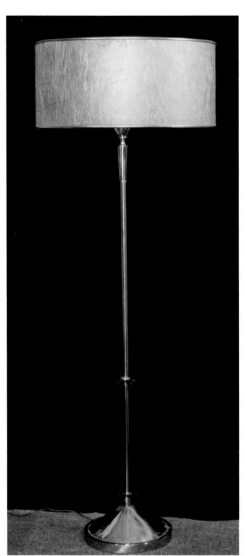

Brass floor lamp. Fiberglass shade. 60". $45-65

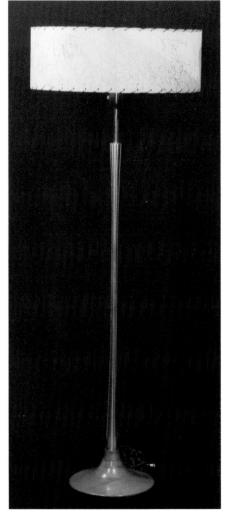

Brass and wood base floor lamp. Fiberglass shade. 60". $75-110

110

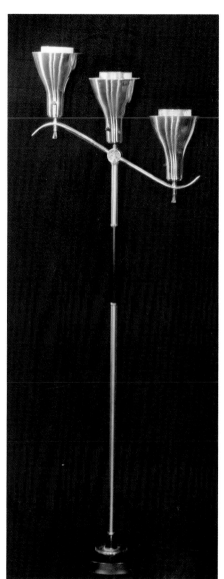

Brass and iron triple shade floor lamp. 60". $95-110

Brass starburst floor lamp. Fiberglass shade. 60" $110-145

111

Brass and ceramic floor lamp.
Fiberglass shade. 60". $75-110

Metal floor lamp with 2 spotlights and
2 tier fiberglass shade. 60". $95-125

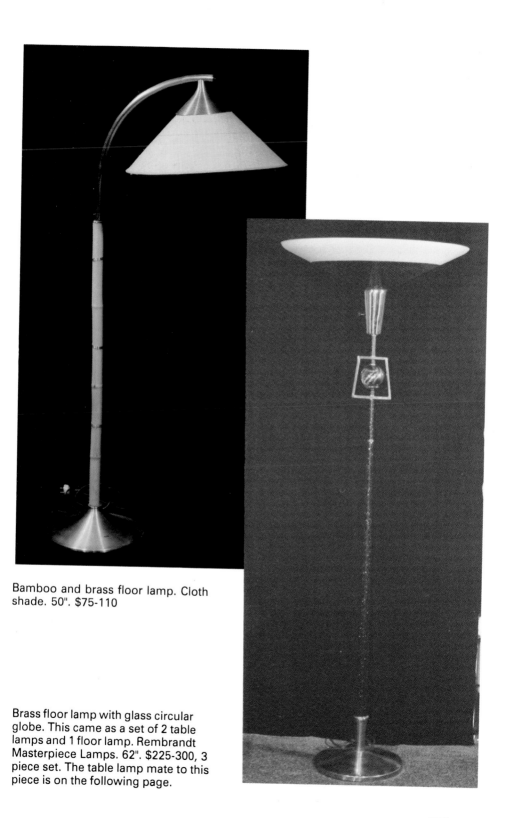

Bamboo and brass floor lamp. Cloth shade. 50". $75-110

Brass floor lamp with glass circular globe. This came as a set of 2 table lamps and 1 floor lamp. Rembrandt Masterpiece Lamps. 62". $225-300, 3 piece set. The table lamp mate to this piece is on the following page.

Brass table lamp. Rembrandt Masterpiece Lamps.

Brass and glass pole light. 8". $65-90

Metal bullet shape lamp. 60". $75-95

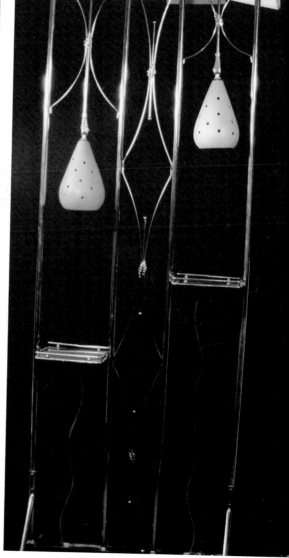

Metal wall divider lamp and shelves.
76". $95-140

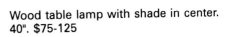
Wood table lamp with shade in center. 40". $75-125

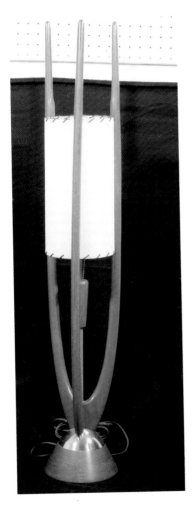

Fiberglass triple globes on stainless steel poles, floor lamp. 60". $100-125

Hanging and Wall Lamps

Plastic grapes hanging light. 14".
$25-50

Plastic grapes hanging light. $25-50

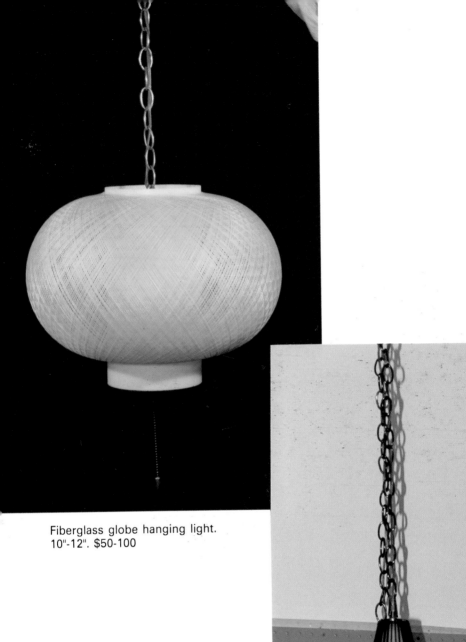

Fiberglass globe hanging light.
10"-12". $50-100

Milk glass hanging light. 12". $50-75

Wood and brass hanging light with triple plastic globes. $50-75

Newspaper advertisement for Lampland, Long Island, New York, featuring two styles of hanging lamps.

119

Glass teardrop hanging lamp from Finland. 14". $50-60

Red glass globe hanging light. 14". $15-35

120

Glass tube hanging light. 18". $70-140

Spun fiberglass hanging ball light.
$45-65

121

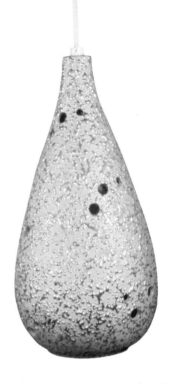

Green moon rock design, hanging
lamp. 14". $40-50

Gold flecked hanging tear drop lamp.
12"-14". $40-80

Spun fiberglass/plastic globe hanging light. 10". $75-150

Wrought iron pin up lamp. Jet black
mesh with parchment shade. 10.5".
$25-35. Top Value stamp catalog,
number 22-2. 1956.

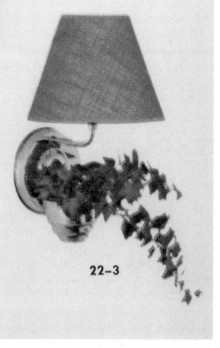

Polished brass planter lamp. Linen on
parchment shade. 10". $25-35. Top
Value stamp catalog, number 22-3.
1956.

Adjustable polished wall lamp. 15".
$45-75. Top Value stamp catalog,
number 22-34. 1956.

Polished brass arm and hood with plastic reflector. Schrader. 13.5". $45-75. Top Value stamp catalog, number 22-47. 1956.

Hobnail milk glass and brass pin up lamp. Rosebud parchment shade. 8". $25-35. Top Value stamp catalog, number 22-48. 1956.

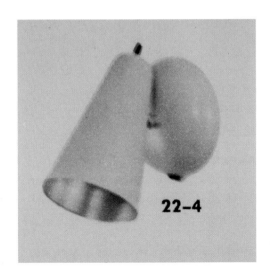

Metal adjustable shade and base pin up lamp. Extends from wall. 8". $18-25. Top Value stamp catalog, number 22-4. 1956.

Desk and Dresser Lamps

Metal phone/clock/table lamp with
venetian blind shade. 15.5".
$150-175

Metal phone/clock/lamp.
Metal shade. $55-75

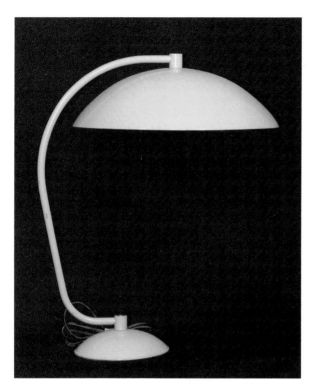

Metal desk lamp. $35-55

Metal desk lamp. 14". $40-80

126

Flying saucer coppertone desk lamp. Came as a pair. 16". $75-125 each

Desk lamp. 12". $40-80

Fiberglass table lamp with double shade. 24". $300-500 pair

Ceramic bulb base table lamp with metal half moon trim. 10". $25-50

Metal and brass dresser lamp with fiberglass shade. 12". $35-65 pair

Brass desk lamp with fiberglass shade. 15". $35-65

Brass adjustable desk lamp with
parchment paper shade. 18" tall.
$35-65 pair

Swing arm desk lamp. Brass with
white boucle over parchment
paper shade. Schrader. 18". $35-65
pair. Top Value stamp catalog,
number 22-46. 1956.

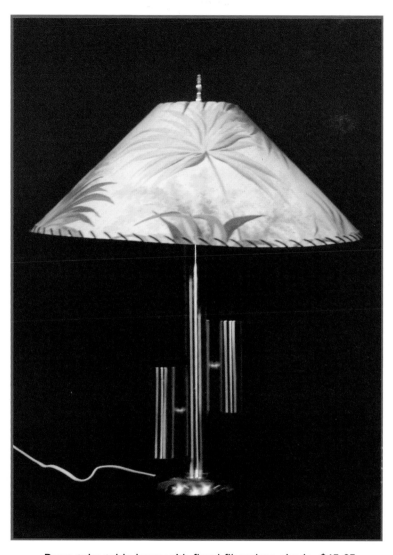

Brass tube table lamp with floral fiberglass shade. $45-65

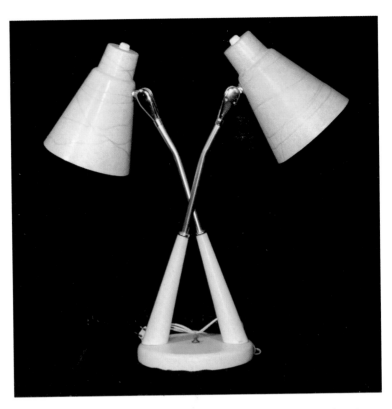

Lucite and metal double table lamp with plastic shade. $45-65

Grecian urn lamp. Brass base. 9". $25-40. Top value stamp catalog, number 22-16. 1956.

Table lamp/planter. Brass base with fiberglass drum shade. Schrader. 25". $35-45. Top Value stamp catalog, number 22-49. 1956.

Brass and copper lamp with metal shade and frosted chimney. 15". $20-35. Top Value stamp catalog, number 22-14. 1956.

22-49

22-14

22-10

Polished base and shade holder. Milk glass shade with star design. 11". $25-35. Top Value stamp catalog, number 22-10.. 1956

133

Colonial, brass trim hobnail glass table lamp with clear glass chimney. 17". $45-65. Top Value stamp catalog, number 22-13. 1956.

Set of boudoir lamps. Milk glass fount and base with polished brass trim, lumarith pleated shade, bow trim. Norman. 17". $45-60 pair. Top Value stamp catalog, number 22-43. 1956

22-43

22-13

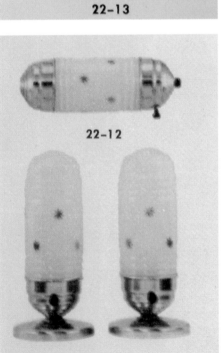

22-12

Vanity lamp set polished brass base with milk white glass globes. 3 piece set. 9.5". $65-95. Top Value stamp catalog, number 22-12. 1956

Miscellaneous Lamps

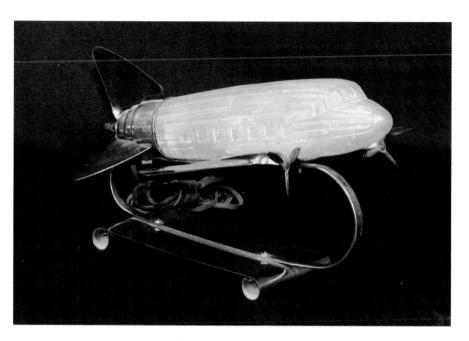

Frosted glass and chrome airplane lamp. 7". $300-500

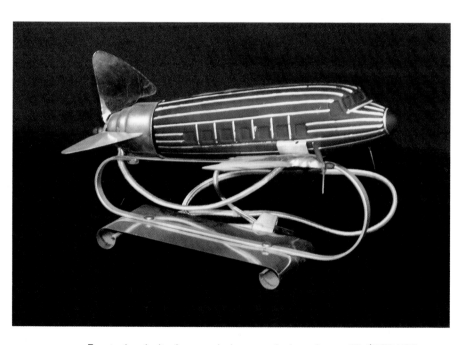

Frosted cobalt glass and chrome airplane lamp. 7". $300-500

Pot metal Statue of Liberty lamp. 11". $50-75

Copper lady holding vase table lamp. 17". $125-250

Green depression glass Saturn table lamp. $300-500

Green depression glass frosted Saturn lamp. $300-500

Van Briggle, Egyptian Goddess table
lamp with plastic double layered
shade. Artist Bill Higman. 1946-56.
$750-850

Ceramic mammy wall lamp with silk
and plastic shade. $125-175

138

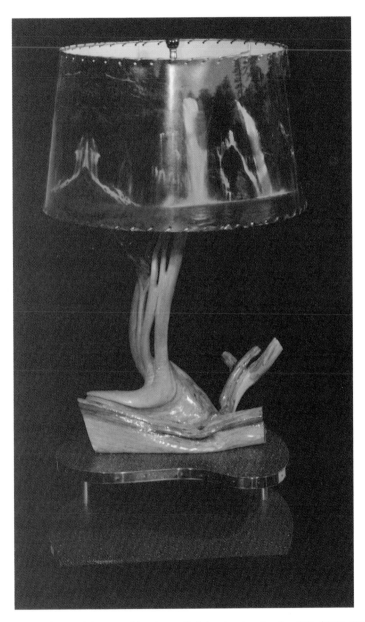

Varnished driftwood lamp with photo finish plastic shade. 29". $100-150 each

Driftwood lamp shaped like a water pump, with plastic western shade. 13". $55-75

Cactus wood table lamp with photo finish shade. $55-75

140

Glass bedroom dresser lamp. 10". $30-45

Plastic candle lamps. $60-90 pair

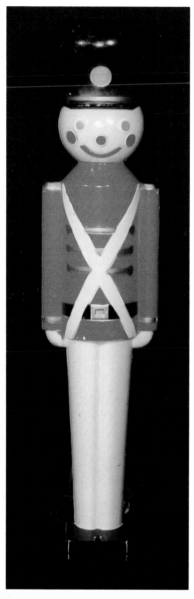

Celluloid standing soldier light. $45-75

Glass pineapple shaped table lamp.
11". $25-50

Cork table lamp with paper shade.
21". $30-55